OBJECT LESSONS
FROM NATURE

OBJECT LESSONS FROM NATURE

by
Joseph A. Schofield, Jr.

BAKER BOOK HOUSE
Grand Rapids, Michigan

Copyright, 1952, by
Baker Book House Company

Taken from 53 *Nature Sunday Talks to Children*

ISBN: 0-8010-8016-9

PHOTOLITHOPRINTED BY CUSHING - MALLOY, INC.
ANN ARBOR, MICHIGAN, UNITED STATES OF AMERICA
1975

Contents

1

"Consider the Years"

(NEW YEAR SUNDAY)

❧〰❧

DEUTERONOMY 32:7—". . . consider the years . . ."

OBJECT—A Calendar.

❧〰❧

THE boys and girls have a text this morning. I think it is a fine thing for the sermon to boys and girls to have a text, just as the sermon for the grown-ups has a text. It helps us to realize how important God's Word is if our sermons start out with texts. It also helps us a little bit to know more of this Book. So our text this morning is from God's Word, from the Old Testament book called Deuteronomy, the 32nd chapter and a part of the 7th verse. Find this verse when you get home, boys and girls. And if you cannot find it alone, ask your father or your mother to help you find it. And some place near the middle of the verse you will read, ". . . consider the years . . ." That's our text and that's going to be our subject, "Consider the Years." And our object this morning is this new calendar for the new year that has just begun. This new calendar will help us consider the years.

New Year's Day was Thursday.* A new year has started. I do not need to tell you that. You know that yourselves. We are already in a new year. A new year has begun.

I

That means that a brand new year is ahead of us. We have just started on it. It has just begun. Except for the two or three days that have already passed, the whole new year is ahead of us. And it will be different. It cannot be exactly the same as last year. It just simply cannot. It is bound to be different from last year and from every other year that has ever been. It just cannot be exactly the same. Every week will be different. Every day will be different.

Why? Why will this be so? Because you will be different. You will be one year older. You will be one year wiser. You will be one year taller. You will be one year different. Everybody around you will be one year different. The world around you will be different by just that much.

II

Now there is something I want to say to you about this new year that is bound to be different. Use it. Use the new year. Use each week of it. Use each day of it. Do not waste it. Do not fritter away, spoil, throw out the days and weeks, the hours and minutes that will make up this new year. Do not waste them. Don't let them slip by unused.

So it was that Thomas Carlyle, the famous English writer, once said,

> "So here has been dawning another blue day,
> Think, wilt thou let it slip useless away?"

* This day, referred to here, may, of course, be changed to suit the particular year in which this talk may be used.

"Blue" here does not mean "sad" as we sometimes use the word; but "clear, bright, beautiful."

> "So here has been dawning another blue day,
> Think, wilt thou let it slip useless away?"

That applies to every day of the year, to every week, to every hour, to every minute; to the year itself. Don't waste it. Don't let it slip useless away. Use the new year.

III

But the new year ought to be the same in some ways. That's the third thing I wanted to say to you this morning. The new year that we have just begun ought to be the same in some ways, in some very important ways. Christ is to be the same Saviour. Christ is to be the same Master. We are to help others, just the same in the new year as we were supposed to do in the year that is past. We ought to serve God in the year that is coming just as much as it was our duty to serve Him in the year that is over. In these ways the new year will be the same as the year that is gone, and these ways are very important ways indeed.

So the new year will be different. But if God was the center of our life in the year that has just ended, the year ———,* and if God is the center of our life in the year that has just begun, the year ———,** the most important parts of the new year will be the same. If God was not the center of life in the year that has just ended, the year ———,* be sure, make perfectly sure, that He will be in the year that has just begun, the year ———.** In the year that is ahead of us, the year that has just opened, the new year, let us make perfectly sure that Christ is our Saviour. Let us be sure that Christ is

* At this point, insert the year that has just ended.
** Here insert the year that has just opened.

our Master. Let us be careful to help others. Let us be certain to serve God.

2

Two Keys on a String

❧～❧

LUKE 22:40—"Pray that ye enter not into temptation."

OBJECT—Two ordinary door keys tied together with a short
length of string.

❧～❧

THERE is a text that I want to give to the boys and
girls this morning. It is found in the Bible, which
is God's Word, in the part of it we call the Gospel according to Luke, the 22nd chapter and the 40th verse:
"Pray that ye enter not into temptation." These words
Jesus spoke to His disciples on the very last night of His
life, when He had gone with His disciples into the Gar-
den of Gethsemane to pray; just a little while before
He was betrayed by Judas, arrested by His enemies,
taken out to a cruel and unfair trial and then put to
death upon the cross. They are very important words
and words which we should remember. Find them in
your Bibles. Luke 22:40. Learn them. Think about
them. Follow them out in your lives. "Pray that ye enter
not into temptation."

I noticed something just the other day, which I want
to try to show to you this morning. I had two ordinary
door keys, like these I now hold in my hand. They were
tied together with a short length of string, as these are
tied. I put the two keys, tied together with string, down

11

upon a table. But I was a little careless as I laid them down on the table and one of them slipped over the edge of the table and hung there in the air, suspended. The other key was back on the table top, some little distance from the edge, and it held the fallen key in the air. The balance was just right. There was just enough string between the two keys and the key lying on the table was just far enough back from the table's edge to hold the fallen key and to prevent it from falling the rest of the way and dragging the other key off the table down to the floor. Let me see if I can repeat the experiment for you on the edge of the pulpit this morning.

See. When I lay these two keys very carefully on the edge of the pulpit, with one key hanging down over the edge and the other lying flat on the surface, the one on top is strong enough to hold the hanging one and keep it from falling to the floor. They are balanced perfectly. But watch! If I give the key on top a little push, if I let it slide a little bit toward the edge, then the weight of the key that is hanging in the air will be enough to drag the key lying flat on the surface of the pulpit-top over the edge and will drag it along with itself down to the floor. The hanging key will pull the other key off and make it fall *only* if the key on top gives in a little bit, is moved a little closer to the edge, slides a little bit toward the key that has already started to fall and would seem to want to drag the other key along with it to the floor. The key on top will fall *only* if it *yields*. And it only needs to yield a tiny bit!

Now these are just two keys on a string. But as I saw this thing happen the other day, I thought that here is a good lesson for us; a simple object lesson but a good one, for boys and girls. Because, suppose we call the one key hanging over the edge, temptation. And suppose we call the other key, the one lying flat on the table top, your resistance. Temptation, the hanging key, is pulling at you all the time and trying to make you fall. Resistance, the key above, is holding you back all the time and is not going to let temptation win. But if resistance gives in a little bit, if you yield to temptation just a tiny particle, then temptation wins and your resistance gives way and over you fall. Temptation cannot ever win so long as resistance holds out. And you know what I mean by resistance. By resistance I simply mean holding out against temptation. And you also surely know what temptation is. Temptation is just a pull on us to do something that's wrong. As long as we hold out against temptation, temptation cannot win. But just as soon as we yield or give in, the slightest little bit; just as soon as resistance gives way, even a little, then temptation wins and over we go!

So the way to resist temptation is not to give in the first little bit. The trouble with a great many people is that they give in from the very start. Some not only give in a little, but go out to meet temptation half way! Some people seem anxious to be tempted; actually go out to meet temptation. And of course, with such people, temptation wins!

There is an old Gospel song your grandparents used to love to sing. Here is the way it began:

> "Yield not to temptation,
> For yielding is sin."

It is no sin to be tempted. We all are tempted to do wrong. Even Jesus, our perfect Example, was tempted to do wrong. It is no sin to be tempted. But it is a sin to yield. It is a sin to give in to temptation. But the song goes on and says next:

> "Each vict'ry will help you
> Some other to win."

Every time you win over temptation you will be strengthened to win again. Don't yield to temptation. Resist. Hold out. Win. And every time you do win, you will be that much stronger to win once more. *Never give in to the Devil*. Remember what Jesus said, "Pray that ye enter not into temptation."

3

From Log Cabin to White House

(LINCOLN'S BIRTHDAY)

❧〜✦〜❧

PROVERBS 3:6—"In all thy ways acknowledge him, and he shall direct thy paths."

OBJECT—A large portrait of Lincoln to display or a quantity of small pictures of him to distribute to the children.

❧〜✦〜❧

IN A LOG cabin, on a farm near Hodgenville, Hardin County, Kentucky, on February 12, 1809, was born Abraham Lincoln.

I

The life and achievements of Abraham Lincoln form one of the glories of America.

Here was a poor boy. He had almost no education. He only had about one year of schooling altogether. Yet he became President of the United States and, many think as I do, the greatest of all Americans.

He moved from a log cabin to the White House. That was a great step. That was a great move. That was a tremendous achievement.

Even the log cabin in which he was born is now covered with a great, beautiful granite memorial building to preserve it always.

This is America. This is one of the glories of our great country. To become great in this land, to become President of our republic, to become one of the greatest of men in this nation, to become, as Lincoln did become, the very greatest of Americans, you need no noble birth. You need no royal family. You need no great wealth. You need no great, important family, like the noble families of Europe and the other countries of the earth. You need no powerful and influential friends. A poor boy can become our greatest man. One can step from a log cabin to the White House. Several of our great Presidents have done that. Abraham Lincoln did.

From a log cabin to the White House is one of the glories of America.

II

It also shows the real greatness of Lincoln.

For Abraham Lincoln, even though he started in a log cabin and even though he had no strong and powerful family behind him and had almost no education and almost no opportunities as we understand opportunities to-day, had great ambition. He studied every chance he got. He borrowed books whenever and wherever he could. He read and re-read the few books he had. There were only a very few that he could either own or borrow. So he had to read them over and over again. He had the Bible, the greatest Book of all, of course. And his study of the Bible was a real education in itself. He read Shakespeare. He had a chance to study Aesop's "Fables." He read "Robinson Crusoe," and "Pilgrim's Progress." He was able to get and study a "History of the United States," and he came to know Weems' "Life of Washington."

And more important than that, he trusted God. He had none of our opportunities to learn of Christ and of God. He had no beautiful Church to attend. He had no Sunday School to go to. He had no Young People's

Fellowship to join. There was no Week-Day Religious Education where he lived. He never heard a Junior Sermon. He had no Junior Church to go to. Yet he trusted God. And that's what made him great.

I am very sure that Abraham Lincoln knew our text of the morning. Proverbs 3:6—"In all thy ways acknowledge him, and he shall direct thy paths." I am sure all through his life he did just that. And indeed that did make him great. In all his ways he acknowledged God and God did direct his paths.

Lincoln was good. Lincoln was ambitious. Lincoln was great. But most of all and most important of all, Lincoln trusted God. And you know I think above all else that is what made him good and that is what made him ambitious and that is what made him great. He trusted God.

"In all thy ways acknowledge him, and he shall direct thy paths."

4

"The Lord Looketh on the Heart"

(VALENTINE'S DAY)

1 SAMUEL 16:7—"But the Lord said unto Samuel, Look not on his countenance, or on the height of his stature; because I have refused him: for the Lord seeth not as man seeth; for man looketh on the outward appearance, but the Lord looketh on the heart."

OBJECT—A heart cut out of colored paper or cardboard.

H ERE is something to look at this Valentine Sunday, boys and girls. You know Valentine's Day will soon be here; and many hearts like this will be seen all about us. Some will be coming to us through the mail. Some will be displayed in stores. Some will be used as decorations for parties. We will be seeing hearts everywhere.

For on Valentine's Day we think of a heart. And a heart stands for love, doesn't it? But the heart also stands for life.

Now there is a text in God's Word which speaks about this very thing, that the heart stands for life. And this text is going to be our text this morning. You will find it in the First Book of Samuel, the 16th chapter and the 7th verse. And this is what you will read: "But the Lord said unto Samuel, Look not on his countenance, or on the height of his stature; because I have refused him: for the Lord seeth not as man seeth; for man looketh on the outward appearance, but the Lord looketh on the heart."

Samuel had been told to find and annoint a King for Israel. God sent him to Bethlehem to the family of Jesse and told him that one of Jesse's sons was to be the new king. And now Samuel was looking over the fine sons of Jesse. And David was the one chosen, the youngest of them all, small and young and weak. Not any of his older brothers, though they were big and handsome and strong. For God told Samuel not to look on the outward appearance but to choose and annoint the one whose heart was right. God would tell him which one to pick, for God would look upon the heart. And God had Samuel choose and annoint David, the youngest, the smallest, the least impressive and promising looking rather than the older brothers, big and handsome and strong.

Your *heart* really shows what you are. Man cannot see it. But God can. And it is your heart which counts. It is your heart which tells. That is exactly what our text is telling us. That is what God told Samuel. That is what Samuel told Jesse. Your heart really shows what you are. Man cannot see it. But God can. ". . . for the Lord seeth not as man seeth; for man looketh on the outward appearance, but the Lord looketh on the heart."

Once there was a slick stock salesman. I knew him. He was big and handsome and smooth. But he had an evil heart. People did not know it at first. But God knew it and after a while people found it out, too. He indeed had an evil heart. For he would steal all that a widow had, all the money that her dead husband had saved up for many years and all she had cared for and preserved for many years after his death. This handsome, tall, fine-looking, smooth-talking salesman would not have stopped until he had taken the last penny the poor widow had by selling to her worthless mining stock. He took her money and he kept telling her he was putting it into a gold mine and that she would very soon get all her money back and much more, besides. But he was really putting it into his own pocket and he never intended her to see any of it again. His outward appearance was splendid. He was big and noble and handsome. But his heart was evil.

Did you ever hear the story of *Cyrano de Bergerac?* It is a most beautiful story by Edmond Rostand; and some day, if you do not already know it, you will want to read it, know it and understand it.

It is a story about a man whose name was Cyrano de Bergerac, a very homely man with a terrible nose. His nose was so large and so conspicuous and so terribly homely that it made him very sensitive. Nobody could look at him but what he thought his nose was being laughed at. So he became very touchy. But he was also very modest. He was afraid to say he was in love with a beautiful lady, because he thought it would be quite impossible for her ever to be in love with a man with such a nose as his. He was very self-conscious. He supposed everybody was looking at him, making fun of him, laughing at his homely nose. So *outwardly* he became very rough, cruel, brutal and wicked. But inside he had a *heart of gold*. He was a good man; a fine man; a loving man; a generous man; a kind man. He would do *anything* for anybody. Outwardly he was most repulsive. But inside his gruff and cruel appearance he had indeed a heart of gold.

So it is the heart that counts. ". . . man looketh on the outward appearance, but the Lord looketh on the heart."

Mind your heart, boys and girls, each of you.
Make it good.
Make it Christian.

5

Bread

(COMMUNION)

JOHN 6:51—"I am the living bread which came down from heaven: if any man eat of this bread, he shall live for ever: and the bread that I will give is my flesh, which I will give for the life of the world."

OBJECT—A slice of bread.

THE text for the boys and girls this morning is from John, the 6th chapter and the 51st verse: "I am the living bread which came down from heaven: if any man eat of this bread, he shall live for ever: and the bread that I will give is my flesh, which I will give for the life of the world." In this text Jesus says that He is the Bread of Life, and those that take of Him will live for ever.

To-day is Communion, and I am glad to see so many boys and girls here, because you can all see what Communion is and can learn much about it so that you will be able to take it when you become members of the Church. For you know that only Church members take Communion. Only our parents and the older boys and girls who are members of the Church eat the little bit of bread and drink the little bit of grape juice that are the elements of the Lord's Supper or the Communion.

Now one of the two elements that Church members take at Communion time is bread, bread broken off from a slice like this. We use just simple, ordinary bread. But bread is very important in life. You know we have to have bread or something of the same nature at just about every meal. And that is why people call bread the staff of life. It is the foundation for all our meals. It is necessary to keep our life going. But when people use the word, bread, they often mean more than just the ordinary bread itself. They use the word to mean all kinds of food. I used to be invited often to come and "break bread" with my uncle and he simply meant to come out to his house for dinner. He used the word, bread, to mean food; all kinds of food; any kind of food they might have that day. And so the Bible uses the word. Bread often means food, and so in God's Book it stands for all that keeps life going; all that nourishes and sustains our life.

During the great Revolutionary War, many, many years ago, there was considerable fighting right here in New York State. And much of it was between the Indians and the white people. The Indians were hired by the British to make all kinds of trouble for the American colonists and they used to come down into the towns and villages without any warning and burn the houses and kill the people. And so the Americans wanted to stop them and sent troops of soldiers into various parts of the state to conquer the Indians. Some of these troops were in Delaware County making an expedition against the Red Men in the Delaware and Susquehanna River valleys and over the hills between the two rivers. Captain Gray, in command of one of the companies, wrote a diary in which he tells of the expedition. In one place he says that the soldiers returned, "almost barefooted and naked; we suffered a good deal for want of bread, as we had not any of that very useful article for four days." * They didn't have any bread for four days and they almost starved! So you see how important bread really is.

There is a story told of Marie Antoinette, the Queen of France at the time of the awful revolution in that country which cost the King his throne, and both King and Queen their lives. Just then the people were very poor and the King was very rich. He had palaces and horses and chariots and fine clothes. Indeed he had all he wanted and many of his people were so very poor that they did not have enough to eat. And the King and Queen did not care. So the people began to complain, and get very restless and it looked as if they would make trouble for the King who lived in luxury while they were starving. Somebody came to the Queen and told her about it and said, "Why, they have no bread to eat!" and the stupid Queen replied, "Then let them eat cake!" She knew so little and was so thoughtless that she supposed if a family had no bread in the house they surely could eat cake. She simply could not understand how anybody could be so poor as to have no bread, to say nothing of cake!

And so the Church members to-day are going to eat the bread of the Communion. And the bread in the Communion stands for Christ given to us. For just as real bread keeps our lives going, so Christ keeps our *spiritual* lives going. When we take Him, we take That which sustains our spirits; That which keeps our souls alive! Christ is the Food upon which our spiritual lives must feed. Christ is the Bread of Life!

* *The Delaware Express,* Delhi, N. Y. My sincere thanks go to the publishers of *The Republican-Express,* its successor newspaper, for permission to quote.

6

The Joy of Being Needed

(PALM SUNDAY)

❧❧

MARK 11:3—"And if any man say unto you, Why do ye this? say ye that the Lord hath need of him; and straightway he will send him hither."

OBJECT—A toy auto.

❧❧

I HAVE a Palm Sunday text for the boys and girls. It is found in God's Word, in the Gospel according to Mark, the 11th chapter and the 3rd verse. "And if any man say unto you, Why do ye this? say ye that the Lord hath need of him; and straightway he will send him hither." I think you will all recognize that text as part of the Palm Sunday story. When Jesus was ready to enter Jerusalem and proclaim Himself King, He needed a little donkey upon which to ride into the city. He sent two of His disciples ahead, you remember, to find the little animal, to bring him out for Jesus to ride on. He told them they would find him tied in the little village ahead of them, that they were to untie him and bring him out to Jesus. And if anybody asked them why they were untying the donkey, they were to say, "The Lord hath need of him."

Here in my hand I have a toy automobile, like many of you children have at home to play with. I brought it with me to-day into the pulpit as our object because I want to tell you about an automobile trip that I had the other day and what happened to me. I was coming home from Watertown,* with my family, and the car needed water. Indeed it needed water so badly that disaster resulted. The car got overheated as cars do sometimes. Something went wrong in the engine and the car got hotter and hotter. Soon all the water in the radiator was boiled out. The Prestone, the anti-freeze mixture that I had in the engine, splashed all over the motor. Smoke poured out from under the hood and came up through the floor-boards into the car. The radiator cap melted. All the oil in the crank-case burned up. The great heat, which boiled out all the water, sent the Prestone splashing all over the engine and burned up all the oil in the crank-case, almost cracked the cylinder heads and almost burned out the bearings. But when the smoke came pouring into the car, I stopped at once, of course. And it was none too soon. It was just soon enough; for a few minutes longer and much more damage would have been done.

We had to be towed into the village of Philadelphia and then we had to wait two or three hours for the car to cool off enough to put fresh water into the radiator and to get started for home once more. That meant that the family did not get home for supper. Worse than that, it meant that I did not get to my engagement that evening. For I was scheduled to speak at a Father and Son Banquet at Richville that evening. But with the car cooling off at Philadelphia, miles away, I just did not get to Richville!

Now will you notice one very interesting thing? All my car needed that day was water. I got into serious trouble—and it might have been much more serious if I had not stopped just the very moment that I did—

* New York

simply because the car did not have water in the radiator! Water is not much for a car to need. You do not even have to pay for water for your engine. It is a small thing, not very much, not very important. But how badly it is needed when it is needed! How badly is water needed by a car going along the road. Just as badly as water is needed by a man crossing a desert. Without water your car will burn up and be useless. Without water a man will burn up and be useless, too. Water is not much. But when it is needed how badly it is needed!

Now it was exactly like that on the first Palm Sunday. The donkey was needed by Christ, the Saviour of men. That little animal was a humble little creature. He was small and unimportant. But Christ needed him. Jesus Christ, the Son of God, the Creator of the world, the Saviour of men, the King of Kings, the Lord of Lords, needed that little donkey.

God needs you. God is so great. He made us and He made the world. We are so small, so unimportant. Yet God needs us. I think that is a wonderful thought. There is a work for each of us to do. There is a place in God's great Kingdom for each of us. Yes, God needs YOU. Give yourself to Him. How happy it will make us when we really realize that God needs us. Think of what that means. God needs you for His purpose and for His Kingdom. No matter how small and unimportant you may think yourself to be, does it not thrill you to think that God—so great, so strong, so powerful, so good, so wise, so loving—needs you? That is the joy of being needed. That joy should be in the heart of every boy and girl. Remember God needs YOU. And remembering that, you will have the joy of being needed.

7

Growth

(RURAL LIFE SUNDAY)

❧

Mark 4:28—"For the earth bringeth forth fruit of herself; first the blade, then the ear, after that the full corn in the ear."

Object—A seed of a Maple tree.

❧

SINCE to-day is Rural Life Sunday, I have an appropriate text for the boys and girls. It is found in God's Word, in the Gospel according to Mark, the 4th chapter and the 28th verse: "For the earth bringeth forth fruit of herself; first the blade, then the ear, after that the full corn in the ear." And I also want to show you this small object I hold in my hand, a seed of a Maple tree. Just a common, ordinary seed of a Maple, such as you see all about you so often, a seed with its two little tails; designed by God to be carried off by the wind and gently planted in some distant spot where it might, with proper moisture and sunlight, take root and grow and eventually become a mighty and a lovely Maple tree.

For as you all know so well, a great tree can grow from such a tiny seed as this. Material is taken out of the ground, out of the air, out of the water to make such a tree grow from such a seed. Is that not a wonderful thing—a miracle? That God can take a little seed like this, make it fall into the ground, make it take

28

root and grow, and from substances already in the ground, the air and the water, change it and develop it into a great and a beautiful tree?

But look at your finger. Here is just as wonderful a thing! Notice how it grows. Notice how what you eat and what you drink, your rest, your exercise, your play make your finger grow with the rest of your body. Think of a tooth in your head! Unlike your finger, made differently, of different material, for a different purpose, yet it, like your finger, grows when your body grows. And exactly the same materials taken into your body—your food, your drink, the rest you take, the sunshine you get, your exercise and all that goes to make your health—combine in some miraculous way to make your finger grow for one purpose and your tooth grow for another! Part of the material that you take into your body turns into your finger. Part turns into your tooth! Growth is a miracle, a miracle of God.

I once knew a very famous American, William Jennings Bryan. He lived many years ago and has now been dead for many years. But I knew him rather well when he was living. He was a very great man. He was one of the three or four greatest orators that America ever produced. You know what an orator is, a speech-maker. And Mr. Bryan was one of the greatest of them. He was the Democratic candidate for President of the United States three times. He was never elected President but he was the candidate of one of the two great political parties in this country at three different times. He was Secretary of State under President Wilson before the outbreak of World War I. He was a Presbyterian Elder, a high honor indeed in our Church. And he was the teacher of one of the world's most famous Sunday School classes, a class in Miami, Florida, that had thousands of members every winter. He was very active, for many years, in the General Assembly of the Presbyterian Church, the national governing body, as you know, of our great denomination. Indeed he was Vice-Moderator (that means, in Church language, Vice-President) of our General Assembly the year before he died. Well, Mr. Bryan, this great American, this great Christian and this great Presbyterian, had a fine old story that he used to love to tell. He used to ask people how it was that a red cow could eat green grass and then give white milk out of which men would make yellow butter. Isn't that a wonder of nature? Isn't that a miracle? How can you account for this combination of colors and this turning of vegetable matter into animal matter? The grass becomes part of the cow. The cow gives the milk. The milk turns into butter. Isn't that a wonderful thing, when you stop to think about it? How is it done?

There is only one answer. There can be only one answer. God does it all. God is the answer. The answer is *God*.

But just think a moment. If God will do this for our bodies, if God will make our bodies grow, will He not also give us spiritual growth? If God makes out of the materials that we eat and drink and breathe, our bodies, strong and big and healthy, will He not also make our minds grow, our characters and our souls? Surely, if we let Him, He will do it. Surely, if we let Him, He will make us like Jesus. Surely, if we let Him, He will make us *beautiful* and *strong* characters.

8

How Wasps Taught Man to Make Paper

(CHILDREN'S DAY)

Proverbs 30:24—"There be four things which are little upon the earth, but they are exceeding wise."

Objects—A small Spruce log or, lacking this, any small piece of a limb or a trunk of a tree; specimens of several kinds of paper, including a newspaper; and, if available, a wasps' nest.

I AM happy, boys and girls, for the opportunity to speak to you on Children's Day. And the subject I am going to discuss is appropriate for this special day and also suitable for this particular year and this particular time. For our county,* you must all know, is 150 years old this year. Of course, the land was always here, but the county was organized as a county 150 years ago. And our village** is taking part in the county-wide celebration. Now paper-making has for many years been a very important industry in Gouverneur. That's why I think our subject not only fits Children's Day but also our lovely village and the historical celebration of which we have been having a part.

* St. Lawrence County, New York, 1802-1952.
** Gouverneur, New York. Both these local references can be omitted when this talk is given. They are included here merely to give local color and to add historical interest.

31

Now this is our text, from God's Word, the Book of The Proverbs, the 30th chapter and the 24th verse. "There be four things which are little upon the earth, but they are exceeding wise." The wise man who was writing says here that there are certain things upon the earth that are very small and apparently unimportant but which are very wise. He says we can often learn from small things. And then, in this same part of the Book of The Proverbs, he goes on to say that ants and conies (animals that may be something like our rabbits) and locusts (a locust is a kind of grasshopper, you know) and the spider are all wise little creatures and they can teach us some things. Have your fathers and your mothers help you find this part of Proverbs when you go home after Church to-day and read four verses beyond our text in the 30th chapter and you will find ants and conies and locusts and the spider referred to. All these little creatures can teach men important things. And so can wasps. In fact, wasps have already taught men something very important. That's our subject: "How Wasps Taught Man to Make Paper."

The story goes something like this. Many years ago, maybe a hundred or so, about the time in fact when our county and our village were rather young, a man whose name was Gottfried Keller was walking through the woods. He was a young German paper-maker. In those days paper was made out of cloth; fine linen or cheaper rags; and it was expensive, because the cloth had to be purchased in the first place and then had to be turned into paper. Well, on his walk, Gottfried Keller kicked a wasps' nest. I suppose the wasps got after him, though I am not sure about that. For the story I read * did not mention that fact. But I suppose they did and you know

* *Pathfinder*, March 20, 1944. Thanks to the publisher for the use of this story.

what wasps can do when they get after a man! So I think Keller must have been pretty sorry for a while that he had kicked that nest. And I do not think he kicked it on purpose, anyhow. But be that as it may, he noticed how the nest was made. It was built of layer on layer of thin, paper-like substance.

He examined it carefully and saw that it was very much like the rag paper that was made at the mill where he worked. He showed it to a friend who knew some chemistry and the two concluded that the wasps made this substance out of Spruce tree fiber. Then they set to work and at last, after much experimenting, they succeeded in making paper out of wood. So pulp paper, as paper made out of wood was called, began.

This made paper cheaper. And it made the large newspaper possible, cheap magazines and cheap books. All kinds of publications could now be made much more cheaply; many more books and magazines and papers could be issued; more people could have reading matter. All because cheaper paper could be made from wood. All because wasps taught man how to make paper.

I

God put wonderful powers in nature and wonderful abilities in animals and small creatures. Wasps can make paper. Bees can make honey. Cows can produce milk. Ants can build wonderful houses for themselves. Birds can build nests.

II

And very often the small and unimportant things can teach us much. We can learn lessons from the squirrel, how to gather and store food. The cat can teach us valuable information, how to take care of oneself, how to keep clean, how to protect oneself. We can profit from the lessons the dog gives to us, the lessons of loyalty and love and devotion. The ant can teach us industry and activity and organization and teamwork. And the wasp how to make paper.

III

God has a place for each of us in this world. God uses the squirrels and the ants and the cats and the dogs for special purposes. God has put us in the world for special reasons, to do particular things, to be useful to Him, to help in His Kingdom. Each of us has a particular reason for being on the earth. Each of us has a place to fill, a work to do. Let us find it. Let us find the place God intends for us. Let us fill it.

That is the message for Children's Day. We may be small and unimportant. But Christ can use us. He has a work for us to do. Let us find it. Let us do it.

IV

And let us ever be ready to learn from others. We should learn from our parents. Our teachers have much to teach us. Even people and things smaller and less important and less smart than we can teach us a great deal, if we are willing to listen, if we are willing to learn. For God teaches them and they teach us.

Do not be too proud to learn from things smaller than you and less important than you. Remember how God said: "Go to the ant, thou sluggard; consider her ways, and be wise." *

* Proverbs 6:6

9

The Moth-eaten Flag

(FLAG DAY)

❧❧

Matthew 6:19—"Lay not up for yourselves treasures upon earth, where moth and rust doth corrupt, and where thieves break through and steal."

Objects—An American flag and a Christian flag.

❧❧

WE HAVE a text this morning, boys and girls. It is found in God's Word, in the Gospel according to Matthew, the 6th chapter and the 19th verse: "Lay not up for yourselves treasures upon earth, where moth and rust doth corrupt, and where thieves break through and steal." This text, notice, speaks about moths corrupting. It tells us that moths do damage. I want to use this verse as our Flag Day text, because Flag Day comes this week, you know.

And I want to tell you a true story. On Memorial Day, a week and a half ago, while the parade was forming on the village parking lot getting ready to march to the exercises at the cemetery, a man who was going to march in the parade told me that he had started to get out his flag that morning and found that he could not display it. It was spoiled and he could not hang it up. It was ruined. Because the moths had gotten into it and they had eaten two of the stripes! That certainly was not a very patriotic thing to do, we both decided. The moths could not have been very good Americans to have eaten two stripes of the American flag!

I asked my friend, "Which color stripes did the moths eat? Were the two stripes they ate both the same?"

And he answered me, "Yes, both the same color. The two stripes that were chewed up were both red."

Why did they choose red? Neither of us could tell. Maybe there was something in the dye that the moths preferred which made them eat the red stripes and leave the white stripes and the blue field. But in any case, the flag was spoiled.

I

Now, why do you suppose moths had gotten into that flag? I don't think we can be sure of the answer to that one. But maybe it was because the flag had not been used enough. We should display the flag often. We, as good Americans, should show our colors. We should be proud of our country and we should show that we are proud of America by displaying the American flag. We should use it often on many occasions. We should show that we are Americans.

But we should also show that we are Christians. We are proud we are Americans. We should also be proud that we are Christians. And we should always be ready to show that pride and display that fact. Show that you are a Christian. Be proud of it. Display it.

II

But maybe the moths had gotten into that flag of my friend because he had not taken proper care of it. Maybe it had been neglected and carelessly put away and foolishly handled and the moths had easily found it and gotten into it and started to eat it. We should take care of our flags, you know. You should take care of the American flag. It is the symbol of the land we love.

But you should also take care of the Christian life; of Christian standards; of Christian ideals; of the things we believe in and stand for. We must preserve these things, too; and take good care of them. Or they will get eaten up! They will get destroyed!

III

Or maybe the flag had not been kept clean and the dirty flag attracted the moths. We should keep a flag clean. It is the symbol of the land we love.

And we should keep our country clean, too. Let us not let evil get into America. When we get a little older and have a little more to say as to how our country is run, let us determine that evils will not ruin America.

And you should keep your Christian life clean, too. Keep your record as a Christian clean.

IV

But remember also, that there is a country greater than ours. I mean God's country, God's Kingdom. Greater than America, more wonderful than America, more lasting than America is God's Kingdom. But that is our country, too. Never forget this. So the Christian flag is our flag, too.

Let God and Heaven have our allegiance, too. We belong to God. Heaven is our final home. Let us always remember that and be loyal. Remember how Jesus said, "Lay not up for yourselves treasures upon earth, where moth and rust doth corrupt, and where thieves break through and steal: But lay up for yourselves treasures in heaven, where neither moth nor rust doth corrupt, and where thieves do not break through nor steal." *

10

Stars

❧❧

Genesis 1:16—"And God made two great lights; the greater
light to rule the day, and the lesser light to rule the night:
he made the stars also."

Object—A large star cut out of cardboard and covered with gold
or silver paper.

❧❧

A BEAUTIFUL and a wonderful verse is our text this
morning. In God's Word as we find it in the Book
of Genesis, the 1st chapter and the 16th verse we read:
"And God made two great lights; the greater light
to rule the day, and the lesser light to rule the night:
he made the stars also."

I have a cardboard star in my hand this morning as
our object. When we make a representation of a star
out of paper or cardboard we usually cut it with
five points as the stars in the American flag are cut.
But I do not want to think to-day of a cardboard star,
but of the real stars in the heavens. One of you has
asked me to give a talk on "Stars" some day. And that
is what I want to do this morning.

Stars are beautiful. When you look up into the
heavens on a dark night, don't you often think how
wonderful the stars are; bright, twinkling, shining
against the black darkness of the night sky? How they
seem to stand out sometimes; how bright they are!
And sometimes they look light bright holes of light,

shining with brilliance as if they were cutting right through a solid ceiling and leading 'way off into the depths of the sky.

I

God made the stars. Every single time I look at one, I think of that. God made the stars. That is what our text said when we began this talk, didn't it? God made the great light of the day, the sun. God made the lesser light of the night, the moon. "He made the stars also." God made the stars; and He made the stars to give us pleasure. He made the stars for us to wonder at; for us to enjoy; for us to delight in.

Did you ever say:

"Twinkle, twinkle, little star,
How I wonder what you are,
Up above the world so high,
Like a diamond in the sky"?*

How beautiful is the star at night! How we do wonder. How we do delight. How truly it does look "like a diamond in the sky."

Well do I remember when I was a student in college. I had a "gym" class late in the afternoon and always, after that class, I would come out of the gymnasium building into the early evening. It was at the University of Pennsylvania in the city of Philadelphia; and as I came out onto the steps of the great, brick gymnasium I often saw the evening star over the dark city, 'way off in front of me, 'way up in the evening sky, with the darkening, growing shadows of the city beneath. And as I stood on those brick steps, looked out over the darkening city and up into the evening sky and beheld that magnificent star shining in all its splendor, I always thought of the great music of the

* Jane (1783-1824) and Ann (1782-1866) Taylor.

great composer: "O Thou Sublime, Sweet Evening Star." For that is just what it was before my very eyes. "O Thou Sublime, Sweet Evening Star."

So God made the stars for our pleasure. But He made them also to make us think of Him. He made the stars to show us His love and His power.

II

Now every time we see the stars, they remind us that God will keep His promises. That is the second thing the stars are always saying to us. First, as I have just said, they tell us that God made them. And then, secondly, they are always saying to us that God will keep His promises.

Did you ever say, early in the evening:

> "Star light, star bright,
> First star I've seen to-night,
> I wish I may, I wish I might
> Have the wish I wish to-night"

and then make a wish on the first star? I used to do that, when I was young. My, it was lots of fun, when we were boys and girls, on a summer evening, very early in the twilight, when the very first, bright star appeared in the sky, to wish on the first star!

But we have something better, much better, than a wish. *GOD HAS PROMISED* and the stars remind us of His promises. God Himself, Who made the earth and the sun and the moon and the stars, has made some wonderful promises to us and He has given us the stars to remind us of those promises. Abraham was promised by God that he would have a family and the promise said that in that family there would be as many people, sons and daughters, grandsons and granddaughters, great grandsons and great grand-daughters, as the stars. There would be as many in the family as the stars! Did you ever try to count the stars? God told Abraham to try. And then he promised him that his family would be like that. And God has certainly kept that promise. For Abraham's family, the Jewish people, are all over the world to-day! There are as many of them as the stars! They just cannot be counted!

So all of God's promises will be kept. God will do what He has promised to do. Just as He kept His promise to Abraham, so He will keep all of His promises. And the stars are to make us think of that!

III

There is a third thing I want to say, a third thing I want you to notice. *Those who serve God will shine as stars.* God calls His helpers and His children jewels. That is a beautiful thought. We read about it in the Old Testament, in Malachi 3:17: "And they shall be mine, saith the Lord of hosts, in that day when I make up my jewels; and I will spare them, as a man spareth his own son that serveth him." A beautiful song has been made about this same idea.

> "When He cometh, when He cometh,
>   To make up His jewels,
>   All His jewels, precious jewels,
>   His loved and His own,—
>
> "He will gather, He will gather
>   The gems for His kingdom;
>   All the pure ones, all the bright ones,
>   His loved and His own.
>
> "Little children, little children,
>   Who love their Redeemer,
>   Are the jewels, precious jewels,
>   His loved and His own."

He will gather His own helpers and His own children; His jewels. And then they will shine like stars.

> "Like the stars of the morning,
> His bright crown adorning,
> They shall shine in their beauty,
> Bright gems for His crown."

The Bible also says that those who serve God, especially those who tell about Him, those who tell about Christ, will shine like stars. "And they that be wise shall shine as the brightness of the firmament; and they that turn many to righteousness as the stars for ever and ever." *

11

Skates in the Desert

❦

Psalm 63:1—". . . a dry and thirsty land, where no water is."

Objects—An ice-skate and a globe map of the world.

❦

IN THE Bible, boys and girls, in the 63rd Psalm and the 1st verse we read about ". . . a dry and thirsty land, where no water is." Now a desert is a dry and thirsty land, where no water is. Our subject this morning is "Skates in the Desert." For I want to tell you a true story; a story about a soldier. He is the nephew of a member of our Church. And it was his aunt* who told me this story, so I know it is true.

Now this young man, about whom our story is told, was a soldier in the Canadian army. On his way overseas, during the great Second World War, he arrived at Halifax, Nova Scotia. Now it seems that he had to remain there at that seaport for some little time, waiting, as we say, to "be shipped across." I suppose the weather was cold. It must have been winter. For, seeing he had some time to wait in Halifax, he wrote a letter home and asked for his skates, so that he could enjoy the ice and engage in the winter sports. Here is an ice-skate. I brought it with me this morning as one of our objects.

---

* Mrs. Aletia E. Davies, to whom I give hearty thanks.

The family, willing to oblige, sent his skates on to him. But he "shipped out" before they arrived.

The ship on which he sailed took him to England. Then he was transferred to South Africa. Then he was sent to North Africa. And all the time, his skates were forwarded to him. They followed him; to England, to South Africa, to North Africa; always just a little too late to catch him. Always they arrived just a little while after he had left. But they caught up with him in the Sahara Desert! At last, the package with the skates arrived. At last the skates caught up with him. And by that time he was in the Sahara Desert, a dry land, where no water is! Hot, dusty, sandy, dry, is the Sahara Desert. There is no ice there for skating!

Our soldier friend had travelled half way around the world. Here, look on this globe as I try to point out to you how he had travelled from Halifax, 'way over here to England, then down here to South Africa and at last up into the Sahara Desert in North Africa.

In that hot, dry, sandy place, he received a heavy package. He opened it. How surprised he must have been to find ice-skates! Of course, he could not use them in the desert, where no water is and where no ice forms. He wanted them in Halifax where it was cold and where there was ice to skate on. He got them in the Sahara, a dry and thirsty land, where no water is! But he had his picture taken putting on the skates in the desert!

I

Now it is important, boys and girls, to *have* the right thing in the right place. Ice-skates in Halifax would have been good. Ice-skates in the Sahara Desert are of no use. Yes, it is important to have the right thing in the right place.

At dinner, we want food. In school, we ought to have pencils and books and there we ought to study. On the playground we ought to have games to play.

Some things we just do not do on God's Day. Some things we do do on God's Day. Some things we just do not do in God's House. Some things we do do in God's House.

It is important to have the right things and do the right things in the right place.

II

But it is also important to *be* the right thing in the right place! If we see some one in trouble, we should be there and *be a helper*. If we discover that some one needs cheer, we should be there, and *be a sunbeam, a bringer of happiness*. There are times and places where each one of us ought to be a helper, a booster, a rooter.

But most important of all, each of us should *be a Christian*. For Christians are needed everywhere and all the time!!

12

41 Wild Flowers in 55 Minutes

(SUMMER)

Matthew 6:28-29—"Consider the lilies of the field, how they
    grow; they toil not, neither do they spin: And yet I say
    unto you, That even Solomon in all his glory was not ar-
    rayed like one of these."

Object—A wild flower.

A T THE Oak Point Junior High Camp this summer,*
I had charge of the Nature Study Hobby Group
several afternoons. On one afternoon, in the hour al-
lotted to us, we went out in search of wild flowers and
flowering weeds. We tried to see how many different
varieties we could find. We walked out along the road
and over the field and up "Angelus Hill" toward the
spot where the Vesper Service was held every evening;
everywhere looking for flowers; bringing them together; comparing them and carefully counting them,
to see how many different kinds we could possibly
find in the short time before we had to return.

We were out on our walking trip 55 minutes, looking carefully about us as we walked, and picking spec-

* Oak Point, on the St. Lawrence River, at the Thousand Islands, near
Hammond, New York. This chapter deals with an actual experience, but
any user of the suggestion back of this story can readily adapt it to one
of his own, fitting circumstances, names of flowers and numbers seen to
his own telling of it.

imens as we went along. We had to be back at our starting point for the next period, so we had less than an hour to be gone. In the 55 minutes that we could use, five minutes less than one hour, we found 41 different types or varieties or kinds of wild flowers; all within sight of the famous old Inn on the bank of the St. Lawrence River. And all of the flowers we found were beautiful. All of them were delicate in form and texture. All were intricate and complicated and wonderful in shape. And all of them were of lovely colors.

We found Daisies and Buttercups and all kinds of Clover, both red and white. We picked Black-Eyed Susans and Wild Asters. We found lots of what we used to call Queen Anne's Lace. We found various kinds of Thistles. And we picked Wild Snap-Dragons, which my grandmother used to call "Butter and Eggs" because of their lovely yellow and orange coloring. And we found many others, the names of which most of us did not know and many of which we had never really noticed before.

But the interesting thing about it all was this. All the specimens we picked were perfect. All the flowers were really beautiful and all were truly wonderful when we looked closely at the blossoms. And there were 41 kinds!

Some were shaped like perfect stars, measuring as much as a half-inch across each blossom; with perfect purple arms jutting out from a center which was a gorgeous yellow tongue. Some were like bells, perfectly formed, beautifully colored, daintily lovely.

Examine a flower closely, some day, boys and girls; one in the woods; even one from the Pulpit bouquet. See how delicate, how perfect it is; how truly lovely!

The whole world about us is beautiful. What is the meaning of all this beauty in the world?

I

God wants us to enjoy life, to be happy, to see the beauty in the world. That's why He made it so beautiful. For us to enjoy! That's an important truth. God made the world beautiful for us to enjoy. That is exactly what Jesus once said, and that's our text for this morning, Matthew 6:28-29: "Consider the lilies of the field, how they grow; they toil not, neither do they spin: And yet I say unto you, That even Solomon in all his glory was not arrayed like one of these." These lilies Jesus knew were wild flowers of Palestine. They grew in the fields, along the roads, on the hillsides. Christ called them "lilies of the *field*," that is to say, flowers that grew wild, out in the country, out in the fields. They were common wild flowers there. And there must have been many different kinds. We do not have some of the flowers of Palestine in our country. But I am sure that many of the flowers we have in America look very much like many of the ones that grow in the land where Jesus lived. And we have many other kinds of wild flowers here in our country. The young people and I found 41 kinds in 55 minutes!

II

Now there is a second thing to say. God wants the flowers and the wonderful things in nature to make us think of Him. We cannot make these lovely flowers. Only God can. So when we see them, we ought to think of Him. What God makes is greater and lovelier than what man can make. Isn't that exactly what Christ meant when He spoke the words of our text? "Consider the lilies of the field, how they grow; they toil not, neither do they spin: And yet I say unto you,

That even Solomon in all his glory was not arrayed like one of these." Nothing Solomon could make was as lovely as the flowers in the field, the common, ordinary, humble wild flowers we see every day growing everywhere.

So the flowers speak to us of God. And as we think of God we worship Him.

> "Joyful, joyful we adore Thee,
> God of glory, Lord of love;
> Hearts unfold like flowers before Thee,
> Praising Thee their Sun above."

So Henry van Dyke sang.* As flowers look to the sun in the sky, our hearts should worship God, our Sun, our Maker, our Saviour, our God!

III

And here is a third thing to think of. God made the flowers. And God takes care of the flowers. Just so, God Who made us, will take care of us. "Are not two sparrows sold for a farthing? and one of them shall not fall on the ground without your Father." ** "Wherefore if God so clothe the grass of the field, which to day is, and to morrow is cast into the oven, shall he not much more clothe you, O ye of little faith?" *** That is Jesus speaking of sparrows and of flowers. We are more important than sparrows or lilies. "Fear ye not therefore," Jesus said, "ye are of more value than many sparrows." **** If God cares for them, the lillies of the field and the sparrows of the skies, He will care for us!

* From *Hymn of Joy* by Henry van Dyke, Charles Scribner's Sons, publishers. Hearty thanks to the publishers.
** Matthew 10:29
*** Matthew 6:30
**** Matthew 10:31

IV

One more thought. Flowers make us think of the beauty of Heaven. When we see God face to face we will be in a world more beautiful, more wonderful, more splendid than this beautiful and wonderful world we live in now. We trust God here. He cares for us. We are to trust Him for Heaven. He will take care of us!

13

Horses

(LABOR DAY)

Psalm 20:7—"Some trust in chariots, and some in horses: but we will remember the name of the Lord our God."

Object—A toy horse or a picture of a horse or horses.

THE first Monday in September is Labor Day. That will be to-morrow. Now Labor Day is a holiday on which we honor all those who work. It is a day set aside in honor of labor. And since men often work with horses, since we think of horses often as work-animals, and since we often measure the work a machine will do in "horse-power," I thought to-day would be a good day on which to talk about "Horses." Besides, one of you has asked me to talk some day on "Horses." And I think maybe Labor Day Sunday is a good day to do it.

Our Labor Day text is about horses. It is from God's Word, the 20th Psalm and the 7th verse. And this is what it says: "Some trust in chariots, and some in horses: but we will remember the name of the Lord our God." And here is the object that illustrates the talk, a toy horse. It is interesting to notice that the word horse or horses is mentioned 221 times in the Bible. I have counted them myself in a concordance (a wonderful book that helps us in Bible study and which I may have a chance to tell you about some day) and so I know this figure is about right. The Bible has a good deal to say about horses.

I

Now horses are handsome animals. Usually they hold their heads high and are proud. Usually they have fine coats and look slick. They prance about with pride and with power. Usually they have a noble bearing. They are fine, splendid, handsome animals.

II

And horses are intelligent animals. I remember some horses very well on my father's oil lease in Pennsylvania. They had been carefully trained by the teamster, who took care of them and also loved them, to take apples and other articles out of his back pocket. And you all have heard of the horse on the old-fashioned milk wagon, in the days when milk was delivered by horse and wagon rather than by automobile as to-day, which knew perfectly well just which houses along the route he was to stop at and which ones he was to pass by. And then there have been many, many stories of the horses in the old days which, late at night, could find their way home without any help from the drivers. Perhaps after some late party somewhere some people would start to drive home. It would be pitch dark. It would be very late at night. But the horse always found his way home. The people in the carriage might even go to sleep, as many of them did! And they would awaken to find horse and carriage and passengers all safely home and standing in front of the barn-door!!

And how these intelligent horses could do tricks in the circus! How well they were trained. How well they acted. How beautifully they performed.

I read the other day about a famous parade in Ohio. It was for some patriotic event. It might have been for Memorial Day or even for Labor Day but it was well advertised and many people lined the streets to witness it. The Chief Marshal, who led the parade, was a distinguished, dignified, handsome man with wavy, white hair. And he rode a beautiful white horse. When horse and rider arrived at the Reviewing Stand, where the judges for the occasion were seated on a platform, a signal was given to the horse to prance higher and thus make the parade more spectacular. But the horse supposed the signal meant to lie down. So he stopped suddenly and as suddenly lay down in the middle of the street and stopped the whole parade and threw judges and marchers and spectators into confusion. He was an ex-circus horse and he thought he was performing for the people instead of mixing up all the plans for the parade!

III

Horses are fine to ride and drive. It is considered great sport to ride horseback and many people still do that very thing and enjoy it tremendously. And to drive a spirited horse along a country road used to be thought of as a very real pleasure, although you see very few horses in traffic these days.

IV

We often hear of horse-power. And it is horse-power, I suppose, that we want to think particularly about on Labor Day as we are talking about horses. For horse-power is a way to measure how much work a machine will do. For example, we say that there are so many horse-power units in a motor; or so much horse-power in an automobile. Horse-power, then, is a very important measurement in figuring out how much work a machine of any kind can do. People interested in machinery are always talking about horse-power.

But we must remember, on Labor Day and every day, that there is also such a thing as man-power. And a man can do more than a horse! Maybe he cannot pull as heavy a load. Maybe he cannot lift as big an object. Maybe he cannot draw as large a cart. But he can do many things no horse can do. So man-power is more important than horse-power.

Also remember boy-power and girl-power! With your intelligence, with your brains, with your minds, as well as with your strength, there are many things a boy or girl can do that no horse could ever do. God gives us our strength as well as our minds and bodies. Remember that when you work and when you labor. Use the strength He gives you for Him! On Labor Day and every day, remember Him who gives you strength and intelligence to labor. Use the strength He gives you for Him.

V

One more thing. Don't trust horses. I mean by that, don't trust in force, in power, in might. Don't put your trust in power. Don't trust in strength. Don't depend on force. Trust in God. That's exactly where our Labor Day text comes in. "Some trust in chariots, and some in horses: but we will remember the name of the Lord our God."

14

A Snowball

(WINTER)

ISAIAH 28:10: ". . . here a little, and there a little."

OBJECT: An imitation snowball made of absorbent cotton.

You know, boys and girls, I think it is fun to take some common and every-day objects and see what they can tell us about life. And because we are in the middle of the winter right now and we see snow everywhere about us, I thought to-day would be a good day to talk about "A Snowball." And I brought a snowball right with me into the pulpit to show you. Oh, no, it is not a real one. I have no refrigerator here in the pulpit in which to keep a real snowball. This is just an imitation, a "pretend" snowball, made out of absorbent cotton. But it will be an object for us to look at to illustrate our subject. And I have a text, too, just as the grown-ups have texts, that will help us think about our snowball. The text is part of the 10th verse of the 28th chapter of Isaiah where it says, ". . . here a little, and there a little."

So this is our object: a snowball. This is our subject: "A Snowball." This is our text: ". . . here a little, and there a little," from Isaiah 28:10.

I

Now the first thing that any one of you would tell me about a real snowball is that a snowball packs. So let's think about that fact first of all. A snowball packs. Every boy who ever made one knows that. Every girl who ever had one fly over her pretty head on her way to school knows that, too. A snowball packs. You can put more and more on it. You can build it up. You can put it together. Because snow sticks together. As you pack it together, the ball gets larger and larger. It is just as our text tells us. "Here a little and there a little." The snowball packs and by putting here a little and there a little you make it bigger and bigger. That's the way you make it. And really that's the only way you can make it.

But in exactly the same way, you can put a little more knowledge onto the knowledge you already have, and sooner or later you will have more knowledge. You can put more and more knowledge together, here a little and there a little, until you have quite a lot of knowledge. You can put more love of God onto more love of God until you possess a great deal of love to God. You can build on what you have. You can pack it together. Knowledge on knowledge; love on love; until you have a great and glorious ball of it. "Here a little, and there a little." And really that's the only way to get it!

II

Now there is a second thing to notice about a snowball. A snowball will break up. You can chip off and off. You can cut a little off here and tear a little off there, until the ball you have built up will now be torn down. The fine, big snowball that you have made will be a tiny, little, no-good pellet.

Just so, you can lose your knowledge and your love of God if you do not use them, keep them together, make them grow. You can chip off a little here and you can scratch off a little there until your knowledge, unused and unappreciated, will vanish away and your love of God, unused and unappreciated, will be no more.

III

I have noticed something else about a snowball. A snowball can turn to ice. Leave a snowball on your front porch some cold night. It will be hard and icy the next morning. It has frozen stiff. Your snow has turned to ice. Your fluffy snowball has turned to a chunk of ice, hard and chill and cruel.

Don't let your religion turn to ice. Sometimes it does, you know. Many a person has let his love for Christ turn cold. Many a person has let his faith grow dim. Many a person has let his religion turn to ice. Don't let yours! Use it. Live it. Keep it warm. Keep it alive. Keep it useful.

IV

A fourth thing about a snowball. A snowball can melt and disappear. Leave it out on your front porch again. But suppose this time the weather turns warm. Suppose a thaw comes and your snowball melts and it is gone! That often happens, doesn't it? I remember how many snowballs I tried to save when I was a boy, only to find them melted and gone the next morning.

Don't neglect your religion. Don't forget it and pay no attention to it. Don't let it melt away and disappear. Use it. Keep it fresh. Keep it growing. Keep it alive.

15

A Meeting in a Haystack

(MEN AND MISSIONS SUNDAY)

❧❧❧

Matthew 13:38—"The field is the world . . ."

Object—A picture of the famous Haystack Monument at Williams College, Williamstown, Mass. If a number of copies of the picture could be secured, on post-cards from a stationer at Williamstown or as prints from a dealer in pictures, the effectiveness of the talk would be increased, as these could be distributed to the children.

❧❧❧

OUR text this morning, boys and girls, is found in God's Word, in the Gospel according to Matthew, the 13th chapter and the 38th verse; the first part of the verse: "The field is the world . . ." I want to use this text for our talk because to-day is Men and Missions Sunday.

This last summer my family and I drove through Williamstown, Mass., where the famous Williams College is located. While we were in that beautiful, little New England town and were looking around the beautiful campus of the college, we visited Mission Park, not far from the college buildings, not far from the main street of the town. In this park we saw a monument.* It is made up of a rather tall stone shaft or column on the top of which is a stone globe, carved like a map of the world. On the monument we read these words: "The Field is the World." Do you recog-

---

* My hearty thanks to Mr. Hiram W. Forbes, Williamstown, Mass., for information about the monument.

nize our text? And underneath, "The Birthplace of American Foreign Missions, 1806." And below this inscription were carved the following names, Samuel J. Mills, James Richards, Francis L. Robbins, Harvey Loomis, Byram Green.

Now there is a story behind this lovely, old monument. And the story is really about "A Meeting in a Haystack."

'Way back in 1806—almost 150 years ago—some young men were students in Williams College who were very serious and devout Christians. They believed that Christ died for them and for all men; and they believed in worshipping Christ and in serving Him. They knew that millions of men and women all over the earth had never heard that Christ loved them and that He died for them. They had never heard this most important of all truths for they had never been told! Nobody ever came to them to tell them! In those days, nobody was going out from America to tell them. There were no missionary societies to raise money to pay the fare of people going out to foreign lands to tell of Christ and to give them clothes and food while they carried on this most important work. There were no Boards or Committees to send missionaries out to China and India and Africa, as there are to-day.

Samuel J. Mills, the young man whose name stands first on our monument, was the man most interested in this and the man who was most distressed when he realized that missionaries were not going out to tell people about Christ in lands where Christ had never been preached. He believed that our country ought to send people to heathen lands to give them the Gospel, that is, to tell them about Christ. So he talked to the other students about his ideas and his anxiety. He prayed with them about the matter. He and a few other young men used to meet together and talk and pray about it.

One day they met outdoors. I suppose it was a particularly good day and they thought it would be fine to have their meeting outside. So they met together in the woods or the field near the college once more to talk the whole matter over. But suddenly a great storm came up. A terrible rain began, with almost no warning, to pelt down upon them. They all ran for shelter. And almost at once they discovered that near them was a large haystack. You know what a haystack is, a great pile of hay carefully piled up in a sort of cone for storage out-of-doors. As soon as the young men saw the haystack, they all scurried under it. And when they were safe and dry under the hay, they went right on and continued their meeting.

They all believed that people should be sent to foreign lands to preach the Gospel of Christ. Each one of them was ready to go himself if some one or some organization would send him. Then they prayed about it. They prayed that God would open the hearts of people in this country to send the Gospel to the heathen. And they prayed that men might be found who would go.

Here began the Foreign Mission Movement in this country, at least as an organized movement with understanding and faith and zeal behind it. For out of this meeting really began the first Foreign Mission Board to be formally organized in America. And some of the men in that very meeting went themselves. Samuel Mills, for example, went to Africa.

So a meeting in a haystack started Foreign Missions in America. I wonder if God did not send that terrific storm at that particular moment for this very purpose. And I wonder if the hay that God had given to the farmer who did not put it in a barn but piled it up in a stack out in the open was not intended to form a meeting-place where missions could get actually started. A storm and a haystack, both gifts of God, both God's handiwork, began foreign missions.

16

"The Flower Fadeth . . . the Word . . . Shall Stand."

(UNIVERSAL BIBLE SUNDAY)

Isaiah 40:8—"The grass withereth, the flower fadeth: but the word of our God shall stand for ever."

Objects—A faded flower and a Bible.

SINCE to-day is Universal Bible Sunday, I thought the boys and girls ought to have a text about the Bible. So I am going to give them one of the best-known and most-loved verses in the whole Book. I shall read the whole verse, and then we shall pick a few words from it to think about especially. The text is found in the great prophecy of Isaiah, one of the greatest books of the Old Testament, the 40th chapter and the 8th verse. I do hope you will look this text up when you get home and that, even better, you will learn it. Here it is: "The grass withereth, the flower fadeth: but the word of our God shall stand for ever." Now I want to pick out the parts of this text that we are to think about especially this morning. ". . . the flower fadeth . . . the word . . . shall stand . . ." Notice them carefully. ". . . the flower fadeth . . . . the word . . . shall stand . . ."

I

Here is a faded flower. Look at it. Note its droop; see its faded petals; observe its lack of color; see its dead appearance; notice the stain and discoloration all about it. Once, not many days ago, this was a beautiful flower. It was fresh and bright and full of color. It had a lovely odor. Its petals stood out, strong and clear and bright. But now it is dead and faded and ugly and done. Once it was beautiful. Now it is anything but lovely.

Beauty is short-lived. After just a little while, it is gone. Yet God gives it. It serves a purpose. It does what God placed it here on the earth to do. Then it is done. Then it is gone.

Life itself is short on this earth. Yet God gives it. God places us upon the earth. And we are here for a purpose. God puts us here, only for a little while, but for a particular reason. There is a purpose in our being here. There is a work for us to do; a job for us to perform; a reason for our creation; a purpose for our being put upon the earth. Let us find that purpose. Let us do it. Let us serve the purpose God placed us here for.

II

Here is a Bible. As you just looked at the flower, now look at the Bible. It is the Word of God.

God's Word lives on. The flower lives but for a day. But the Bible lives for all time. ". . . the flower fadeth . . . the word . . . shall stand . . ."

Isaiah, the great prophet, wrote that text over 700 years before Christ was born on the first Christmas day in far-off Bethlehem. Christ was born about 1955 years ago. So this great statement of Isaiah's must be at least 2655 years old. How many flowers have come and gone in that time? Millions and millions, of course! And they all have faded and passed away and are gone. But the Bible still stands! ". . . the flower fadeth . . . the word . . . shall stand . . ."

People have tried to destroy the Bible. Over the years they have tried in many different ways and they have tried very hard. Years ago, men who wanted the Bible destroyed used to build great bonfires in which they hoped every single copy of the Book would be burned up. Men who translated the Bible into the language of the people were burned at the stake. Do you know what that means? That means that they were tied to a great post so that they could not get away and then a great bonfire was built around the bottom of the post and they were burned to death! People who loved the Bible, God's Book, had to hide it in those days. They had to read it in secret so that the police would not find it and take it away from them and destroy it. Some even baked the Bible in bread to hide it from the soldiers.

Yet the Book is still here. And it will live on.

III

Heaven is ahead of us, boys and girls. Heaven is beautiful like a flower, only more so. We really cannot understand how wonderful and how beautiful and how glorious heaven must be. That's why I say if a flower is beautiful, heaven must be much more so. And heaven is promised to us in the Bible. Do you see how I am connecting heaven with the flower and with the Bible? Heaven is more beautiful than any flower. Heaven is promised to us in the Bible. The Bible gives us heaven.

And the beauty of heaven will never fade. We are

to live for ever in heaven. So in this respect heaven cannot be like a flower. For a flower fades and heaven will never fade. In this respect, then, heaven is like God's Word. For ". . . the word of our God shall stand for ever." And it is that same Word, that Word that shall stand for ever, God's Word, that promises heaven to us.

The flower fades and is gone. We are to live for ever with God. His Word promises it. His Word cannot fade. His Word shall stand for ever.

17

Lost in a Great City

(UNIVERSAL BIBLE SUNDAY)

❧

Isaiah 30:21: "And thine ears shall hear a word behind thee, saying, This is the way, walk ye in it, when ye turn to the right hand, and when ye turn to the left."

Objects: Any sign-board or traffic direction-pointer, or a cardboard imitation of one and a Bible.

❧

Since to-day is Universal Bible Sunday, the boys and girls have a Bible Sunday text. It is found in the Bible, God's Word, in the book of Isaiah, the 30th chapter and the 21st verse. "And thine ears shall hear a word behind thee, saying, This is the way, walk ye in it, when ye turn to the right hand, and when ye turn to the left."

I

Many years ago, when I was a small boy, my sister and I were in the City of Philadelphia with our family, visiting at the home of my grandmother, who lived in the very heart of the old city. While we were there, we were taken out into the country to spend a few days with an aunt, who lived thirty or forty miles outside the city. When our visit in the country was over, we two children came back by train into the city alone. We were to be met by relatives in the great, old station, located in the very center of the city and called Broad Street Station. But when we got off the train, and came on through the great, old station, we did not find the person who was to meet us there and take us home to grandmother's house. Something had gone wrong and he was not at the station to meet us.

We waited around a little while, and then decided that we could find our way by ourselves. Grandmother's house was not very far away and it always had been a short, easy walk from the station to her home. Now there was a short cut, up one street, across another, over another and around a corner and there you were! But my sister and I decided not to take that short cut that day. It went across and around several different streets and we were afraid we would miss it and get lost. You see, we were not too sure of the short cut; but we knew that if we walked north up Broad Street until we came to Vine and then turned left on Vine Street and walked west on that street we would come to the house. The station was called Broad Street Station. It must surely be on or very near Broad Street. All we needed to do, then, was to find Broad Street and start walking.

So I led the way, for I was older. We found our way to the City Hall, which building I thought I knew pretty well. Now we knew that City Hall in Philadelphia is located exactly where Broad Street crosses Market

Street. In fact, both streets have to go around it, for the great building is built right on the intersection. So we made our way to City Hall, went through the passage in the building that led to the great central, open court. This is a large open square, with the massive building on all four sides of it and with passages or tunnels leading out in each of the four directions, right through the building on each of the four sides so that people on foot can walk out of the central court of the building either north or south on Broad Street or either east or west on Market Street. So far, so good. We were safely in the great open court in the middle of City Hall.

But here is where we made our mistake. We turned south instead of north onto Broad Street! You simply cannot do that now. That mistake cannot longer be made. Because the four passageways are clearly marked. Over one a sign reads, "Broad Street, North." Over another, "Broad Street, South." And over the others, "Market Street, East," and "Market Street, West." But in those days, so long ago, there were no signs over the passageways. So we turned in the wrong direction. We walked south, down Broad Street, instead of north.

And we kept on walking. The more we walked, the more tired we became. And the suitcase got heavier and heavier! We had a lot of fresh pears inside that my aunt had given us to take along when we had started to return to grandmother's. My! How heavy those pears inside that suitcase got! And the worst part of it was, that, while we looked at the street signs at every corner, we never came to Vine Street! Farther and farther we walked, getting more and more weary and wondering more and more why we never came to the right corner.

Finally, after we had walked many blocks south instead of north, we stopped and asked a postman if he could please tell us how to get to Vine Street. And he told us we were walking in the wrong direction! He told us to turn right around and walk north instead of south and just about as many blocks *north* of City Hall as we were then *south* we would come to Vine Street.

So we turned around and walked back. After a while we came to City Hall. We walked right through it, through one tunnel or passageway into the great, central court and through a second one onto North Broad Street. On north up Broad Street we walked, block after block, until at last we came to Vine. Then we turned left and started walking west.

And still that suitcase loaded with pears grew heavier and heavier.

A kind man was sitting on the front steps of his house along the street. He saw us pass and noticed how hard it was for me to carry the heavy suitcase. He called to me and suggested that if I wrapped my handkerchief around the handle of the suitcase it would prevent the sharp, metal handle from cutting my hand. I was very grateful to him for his kind and thoughtful suggestion. And at last we arrived, very late, very tired but very grateful that we had finally found the way.

Now you see the real trouble was that we had needed a sign-board or a direction-pointer to show us the way. If the direction had been marked inside that City Hall courtyard, as it is now, we would not have turned in the wrong direction, we would not have become lost in a great city. What we needed was a sign that told us which way to go. Something like this one that is used on our streets and highways to tell people which way to go and which way to turn. We needed the kind of thing that the text of the morning was talking about, something that would say to us, "This is the way, walk ye in it."

II

Now just as we got lost in the city, so people get lost in life. All of us at times get mixed up, go the wrong way, do not know what to do next. We get lost in life. "What should we do next?" we ask. "Which way shall we turn?" "What is right?" "What is wrong?" All through life these questions come up and over and over again we are looking for the answers.

Where can we find the answers? Where can we find a guide-book for life? Where can we discover a sign-board? Where can we see a direction-pointer? The Bible is the answer. The Bible is the guide-book of life. The Bible is the sign-board that tells us what to do next, where to turn, where to walk, what is right and what is wrong.

That is just what our text is telling us about our lives. "And thine ears shall hear a word behind thee, saying, This is the way, walk ye in it, when ye turn to the right hand, and when ye turn to the left." This word that tells us, "This is the way, walk ye in it, when ye turn to the right hand, and when ye turn to the left" is the Bible. The Bible is the sign-board of life. The Bible is the direction-pointer.

It will keep us out of trouble. It will show us the dangers to avoid. It will put us on the right way. It will point us home to God!

18

The Sensitive Plant

❧❧❧

OBJECT: If a specimen of a true sensitive plant cannot be obtained from a florist or a botanical hothouse, a small branch of almost any shrub or tree having pinnate leaves (as the locust tree) would do very well to give the general effect of the appearance of the sensitive plant.

❧❧❧

D ID any of you boys and girls ever hear of a sensitive plant? For there is such a thing. Indeed there are several varieties of plants that are called by this name because of the sensitive way in which their leaves behave. The true sensitive plant is called by the technical, botanical name of *Mimosa pudica*. It looks very much like this branch of the locust tree I hold in my hand but it is a small shrub growing a foot or so in height and found only in hot countries or in hothouses. It has a long, graceful leaf, shaped something like a feather, and divided into many small parts or leaflets. Whenever a leaf is touched, it begins to close up, the small leaflets that make the bigger leaf closing together in pairs until the whole leaf is closed up as if it were asleep. If the leaf is touched often or roughly, the other leaves on the plant near it will also begin to close up. And if the main stem of the plant is violently shaken, all the leaves on the entire plant will begin to close, lop over and hang down as if they were withered. After a time, if the plant is left alone, the leaves will begin to lift themselves up, the tiny leaflets will open once more, and the plant will come back to its original or normal appearance. Now the real sensitive plant acts very quickly when it is touched. But there are several other kinds that act in much the same way even though they may do so more slowly and not so completely. But we call them all sensitive plants, because they close up their leaves when they are touched.

But you know some people are like the sensitive plant. Some people are very sensitive. Often we call such people "touchy." They get upset, they get angry, they get hurt, they get what we call "mad" at a touch. And sometimes we see people who are very sensitive or touchy, who get angry or hurt at the slightest touch. Others take much longer to react, much longer to get angry or hurt if they are touched. You have seen such people. Perhaps you yourselves have acted that way many times.

Now I do not mean that we really touch such people with our hands. It may be that we say something they do not like. It may be that we forget to say some word that they think we ought to say. It may be that we do something that they do not think is just right. And because they are sensitive people, because they are touchy, they get angry, or they get sulky, or they get obstinate, or they get cross. They are like the sensitive plant, irritable and touchy.

But the worst thing about it is that they close up when they are irritated, just like the plant closes up; and like the plant, they no longer show their true selves. Touchy people, irritable people, sensitive people, close up like the leaves of this plant and do not show themselves at their best. Their true selves, their best selves, their real selves are covered up and something false and mean and disagreeable is seen instead.

Let us not be that way. Let us not be like the sensitive plant, beautiful and lovely until touched, and then limp, and glum and gloomy and disagreeable. Let us not be touchy. Let us not be sensitive. Let us never be like the sensitive plant!

19

Sailing

❧ ♡ ❧

2 CHRONICLES 25: 19: ". . . abide now at home . . ."

OBJECT: A toy sailboat or a picture of a sailboat.

❧ ♡ ❧

B OYS and girls, we have a text this morning, from the Word of God, in Second Chronicles 25: 19, the middle of the verse, ". . . abide now at home . . ." Just remember that text, please, for we shall come back to it in a little while. ". . . abide now at home . . ."

I read a lovely little rhyme the other day about a boy sailing a toy boat. And now I want to read it to you. It is called, " Sailing." And this is the way it goes:

> " Oh, if I had a real ship,
>   I'd sail so far away
> I'd not come back till awfully late,
>   Or maybe the next day.
>
> " I'd sail from here to Hudson Bay
>   Or maybe Puget Sound;
> But when the dark of nighttime came
>   I think I'd turn around;
>
> " For who'd be there to tuck me in
>   And hear me say my prayers?
> I guess I'll stay right here at home
>   And go to sleep upstairs! " *

* From " Happy Hours " by Elizabeth Daniel. Copyright 1934 by Rand McNally & Company. My sincere thanks go to the publishers for their kind permission to use this poem.

Don't you like that little poem? I do, very much! Because it makes me think so much of you and of me! For boys and girls are just like that, aren't they? You and I are just like that little boy sailing his toy boat on the little brook and thinking of sailing 'way off, far from home, clear across the world, but coming home to go to bed at night!

Sometimes we think we'd like to wander far away; take great long trips and see wonderful sights all around the world. And it would be a wonderful thing to see the world, wouldn't it? But when night comes, we are very glad to be at home. When it gets dark and the sun has gone down, and we begin to get sleepy, there is no place like HOME. Home is the place we want to be.

And sometimes we are even tempted to run away. We think something has gone wrong at home. We think we are not treated just fairly. We get the idea we are abused and we decide to run away from home. I think most boys and girls sometime or other in their lives get the notion that they want to run away. I remember that I did once. And so I started out and I got six whole blocks from home, down to the old bridge that crossed the river. That seemed like a very long distance from my home. And then it started to rain. The sky became very dark. The rain soaked into my clothes. Night was coming on. I was only a little boy. And I decided to go back home. No more running away for me! I had had enough. Back home I went.

Boys and girls, we should be ever so thankful for our homes. And for our parents who love us. Think how much we owe to them. Think how much we owe to our homes, warm and safe and comfortable and secure! How grateful we ought to be for our homes and for our parents who provide everything for us!

Be loyal to your homes, boys and girls; be true to them. And each boy or girl who has a good home ought not only to be loyal to it and true to it and grateful for it, but he should be in it often. Be glad you have a good home. But more than that, take advantage of it by being in it and by enjoying it. Be there often. Be there much. For the day will come when you cannot be in it any more.

And do your part in your home. There is a work for each of us to do. And as you realize how much your parents do for you in giving you a good home, you in turn should resolve to do your part in making the home pleasant and attractive and beautiful. Do your part to make your house a home!

Be proud of your homes, boys and girls. They have given you much. You owe much to them. Be proud of them! APPRECIATE THEM!

And that brings us back to our text. I have just been trying to tell you that we all should be thankful for our homes, be loyal to them, be proud of them, appreciate them, do our part in them, be in them often. So you see where the text fits in, for it says: ". . . abide now at home."

20

*One Little Lamb**

(MOTHER'S DAY)

❧

2 SAMUEL 12:3—". . . one little ewe lamb . . ."

ISAIAH 66:13—"As one whom his mother comforteth, so will I comfort you . . ."

OBJECT—A carnation.

❧

TO-DAY, boys and girls, is Mother's Day. It is the day on which carnations are worn. People wear carnations this day to honor their mothers. A person wears a colored carnation if his mother is living and a white one if his mother is dead. It is a day on which we honor our mothers.

I want to read you a text this morning, from the

---

* The true story which is the basis of this sermon was told to me by Mr. George A. Lockie, an Elder in the First Presbyterian Church, Gouverneur, New York. He is the owner of the flock and the shepherd in the story. My thanks are extended to him both for the story itself and for permission to use it here.

Word of God as it is found written in the Second Book
of Samuel, the 12th chapter and the 3rd verse. Just part
of the verse is our text; the part which reads, ". . . one
little ewe lamb . . ." And I read that text because I
have for you a true story for Mother's Day, a story
about "One Little Lamb." One of our elders is a wonderful sheep raiser. What he does not know about sheep
is not worth knowing. He loves them and he cares for
them and he has wonderful success with them. And
the story I am going to tell you he told me himself
and the sheep owner, the sheep raiser, the shepherd in
the story is the man himself who told me all about it.

This spring one of the sheep of his flock, a ewe
sheep, that is a mother sheep, had one little lamb. But
the little baby lamb was not very strong and not very
healthy and he died. The mother sheep stood by it,
bleating as if her heart would break. Her little baby
was dead and she would not be comforted. The shepherd hid the body of the little dead lamb, so that the
grieving mother could no longer see it; and he waited
to find out if, when the dead body was taken away, the
mother sheep would forget her loss. But no. Still she
would not be comforted.

Now there were a good many other lambs born into
the flock about that time. Many of the other sheep mothers were having babies, too. There was one particular ewe
mother which had three lambs at once, tiny little trip-
lets. Usually, when lambs are born, there is only one
or at most two. But this mother had three babies. And
that is a big family to be born at once. And one of these
little triplet lambs was very small, puny and weak. He
could not fight the other two triplet lambs to get at
the mother's milk. They were always there first. And
they were always pushing him aside. And so the poor
little fellow did not get enough to eat and he kept

getting weaker and weaker and very soon he was in very great danger of starving to death.

The shepherd felt that here were two problems on his hands. There was the mother sheep mourning herself sick over the death of her little lamb. And there was the third little triplet lamb, ready to starve to death because he could not get at his mother's milk. What a fine thing it would be if the motherless little lamb would only be adopted by the mother whose baby had died. Then the mother would have a lamb to love and the little, starving lamb would have a mother who would love it and care for it. So the shepherd took the little, hungry lamb to the grieving mother, hoping that the two would get along together and all would be well. But the sorrowing mother did not know the new little lamb. She smelled of it. She carefully looked it over. But it was not hers. It was not the lamb she had lost. It was not her baby. And she turned her back upon it and would have nothing to do with it. It did not belong to her and she would not have it! She turned away. She would not feed the little one. She would not let him come near her. She pushed him aside. She would have nothing to do with him. He was not hers and she would not take him.

What was the shepherd to do next? The mother sheep would grieve herself to death. The baby lamb would die of neglect and starvation. Something must be done.

So the owner of the flock skinned the dead lamb, the baby of the sorrowing mother. He trimmed all the meat away from the skin he had removed from the dead lamb very carefully. He cut the skin down to size. And then he tied the skin of the dead lamb over the little, weak, living lamb; and fastened it securely with strings around the neck and the legs. Then he took the sick, weak little lamb in the skin of the dead lamb and brought him to the mourning mother which had lost her baby.

She jumped at it as if her own dead lamb had come back to life. She smelled the skin. She believed the little lamb to be her own. She cared for the little one. She fed him. Carefully she protected him. She looked out for him, kept her eye on him, hovered around him. She adopted him as her very own.

And the little one grew and thrived. All were happy. His life was saved. Her sorrow was over.

After several days, during which the mother sheep tended to the little lamb with all her care and all her love and during which the tiny, sickly little fellow began to grow and strengthen and improve and frisk about like any little healthy lamb, the owner cut away the false skin from the body of the baby lamb. For now he was no longer an outcast and a stranger. Now he belonged. Now he was the lamb of the adopted mother.

Here is a story to show the instinct of mother love. The mother sheep loved her little lamb. She mourned when he died. And when she was given another one and came to think of it as her own, she cared for it, nourished it, fed it, protected it and brought it up as her very own. She gave a mother's care to a little lamb even though it was not her own. She had mother love in her make-up and she showed it to the little, needy one.

Our mothers are like that! They care for us, they protect us, they feed us, they love us, they bring us up. They do all this for us, whether we are their own or whether, as in so many cases, we are adopted.

But often mothers need help. The mother sheep needed the owner of the flock to help her; to give her a lamb to love when she had lost her own. So our mothers need God to help them.

Our mothers explain to us how much God does for them and for us. God gives us life and food and shelter and a home and clothing. God gives much to our mothers and they give much to us. Thus they in turn help God. For you see they really help God care for us, bring us up, feed us, protect us, help us. Mothers and God work together. Mothers help God as He gives life and all things to us.

Thackeray, one of the greatest of all writers, said in *Vanity Fair,* one of the greatest of all books: "Mother is the name for God in the lips and hearts of little children."

God and Mother look after us. Mothers are God's helpers. And God is the Helper to all good mothers.

So I want to read you a second text before we stop. I turn to God's Word a second time; this time to the great Prophet Isaiah, the 66th chapter and the 13th verse. And here we read: "As one whom his mother comforteth, so will I comfort you . . ."

God loves us, cares for us, looks after us, helps us like a mother. God and mothers work together!

21

The Persistent Little Mouse

❦

2 TIMOTHY 4:2—". . . be instant in season, out of season . . ."

OBJECTS—A metal waste-basket and a yardstick.

❦

THE boys and girls have a text this morning. They have two objects to look at. And they have a true story. This is the text, from 2 Timothy 4:2, ". . . be instant in season, out of season . . ." What does that text mean? Just this. Work at it all the time, if you are doing a thing worth while. If the thing you are doing is worth doing, keep at it, work at it, keep it up. Be instant in season, out of season. Keep at it all the time and get the job done.

Now here is the true story and here is where the two objects come in. While I was a student at Princeton Theological Seminary, I used often to see a little mouse try to get something to eat. He was a cute little fellow. He reminded me so much of the little mouse that Robert Burns, the great Scotch poet, talked about in one of his famous poems. He called his mouse a "wee, sleekit, cowrin, tim'rous beastie." * And the mouse that used to visit my room was also a "wee, sleekit, cowrin, tim'rous beastie."

I, like all students away from home at school or college, had thrown empty cracker boxes, candy-bar wrappers, fruit skins and such things into my waste-basket near my desk. And I suppose the mouse, who must have had a good sense of smell, learned that such remains of food were in the basket and was very anxious indeed to get at them. He thought he knew where he could get something good to eat. Now he was a little, tiny mouse and it did not take him long to find out that he just could not climb the steep, straight, metal sides of the waste-basket and get in. The basket in my room was much like this one that I hold before you. He could not gnaw through the sides. He could not climb up the sides. But he wanted the food and he was going to get the food and he was not going to let the metal waste-basket stop him. What do you suppose he did?

Well, I will tell you what I saw him do. When he saw he could not get directly into the waste-basket, he ran over to an open bookcase that stood near my desk and about three feet from the waste-basket, about the length of this yardstick away. Then he climbed up the leg of the bookcase; then he climbed up the edge of the books on the bottom shelf of the bookcase. Then he ran along the top of the books and took a great leap across space to the basket. He often missed, for that was a long leap for a little mouse. He landed on the floor instead of inside the basket. But he would try again. He would run back to the bookcase, up the leg, up the edge of the books, across their tops to the side nearest the waste-basket and try another leap. If he fell

* *To a Mouse*, 1785

onto the floor he would try again. If he failed he would try once more. Over and over he tried; again and again he made the leap; again and again he would have to run back and start the process all over. But at last he made it. At last the jump was long enough; and he landed exactly where he wanted to be, right in the middle of the waste-basket and his reward! And then he would scurry around in the basket, rattling the papers inside, hunting for crumbs and eating everything he thought looked and smelled good. He had to make many attempts, but at last he got there.

Now here is a moral from a mouse. Keep at it. Don't give up. If the thing you are doing is worth doing, keep at it. If the thing you are doing is right, don't get discouraged. Try and try again. You may not make it the first time and you may not make it the tenth time. But you might make it the eleventh or the fiftieth. The little mouse was persistent. He kept at it. He tried over and over again. And at last he succeeded. So can you, if you keep going. Don't give up. Keep at it.

22

The Frying-Pan

MATTHEW 12:45: ". . . the last state of that man is worse than the first."

OBJECT: A frying-pan.

O UR text this morning, boys and girls, is found in the Gospel according to Matthew, the 12th chapter and the 45th verse. ". . . the last state of that man is worse than the first." In these words, Jesus was telling about a certain man who became worse off after a certain thing happened than he was before. I am not going to tell you about the man Jesus was talking about. But I do want you to notice that in one place He told about a person who became much worse after a thing happened than he was before.

And the object I have with me this morning for our object lesson is this frying-pan.

I

Notice this frying-pan. It is a useful object. It was made for a purpose. And in serving the purpose for which it was made, it becomes a very necessary and a very useful article in every house. I certainly think that no housewife can keep house without a frying-pan. All of you have seen such a pan in use on your mother's stove again and again, I am sure. A frying-pan, then, is a useful object. It was made for a purpose.

But, boys and girls, so are we. We were made for a purpose. We ought to be useful. Let us do the thing we were made for.

God put us on this earth. You all know that. And He wants us to do the particular job He plans for us. Let us find it and do it!

II

Now the frying-pan has a second thing to say to us. Don't go from where you are to something worse. Just hold on a minute and you will see how it is that this frying-pan is saying this to us. But first let us make sure what it is the pan is saying. It is saying, "Don't go to something worse." Maybe you are not satisfied with things as they are for you. Maybe you have a hard job to do. Maybe you find yourself in a hard place to be. But the pan is saying to you all the time, "Don't go to something worse."

There is an old saying, you know, "From the frying-pan into the fire." * It means, of course, that it is foolish for us to go from one bad thing into a worse thing; to

* John Heywood, c 1565: Proverbs: Part ii, Chap. v. Also Miguel De Cervantes, 1547-1616: Don Quixote: Part i, Book iii, Chap. iv.

go from one state that is undesirable into a position or state that is more undesirable. I think that is exactly the kind of thing Jesus was talking about in our text, when He spoke of the man who went from bad to worse; from one thing that was bad enough to another thing that was worse. You remember Christ's words that I read to you. "The last state of that man is worse than the first."

Be sure that your move, whatever it may be, is good and not bad. Don't jump from the frying-pan into the fire. If you are going to make a change of any kind, be sure you do not make a change for the worse.

III

Now there is a third thing that the frying-pan says to us, if we will but listen. Appreciate what you have. You may not have much, but appreciate what you have. If you have only a frying-pan, be glad. That, at least, is a start!

There is an old story about a tramp who went to a certain farmhouse one summer day. He was torn and tattered and he was as hungry as hungry could be. But he said to the woman at the farmhouse that he would like very much to borrow a kettle from her so that he could make himself some stone soup. My, he was hungry, he told her. But he would not ask for anything but a kettle, and he would soon return that. He could make himself some stone soup.

"Stone soup? What good is that?" the woman asked.

"Just you wait and see," the tramp replied.

So he took his borrowed kettle, went out to the field and selected a big round stone, washed it carefully in the little brook, put it in the kettle, covered it with water, built a kind of camp-fire with a rack of sticks over it and hung the kettle over the fire to boil.

Then he came to the house and asked the kind lady to give him a little salt to flavor his soup so that it would not be too flat. He really needed some salt to complete his stone soup, but that would make it perfect, that would be all he needed, that would be all he would ask for. But in a few minutes, he came back once more and asked for a carrot to go into his stone soup. After a little while, he returned and requested a potato. Soon he was back again for an onion. Still later he asked for a little piece of meat. And before he was done with it, his stone soup turned out to be a pretty good meal!

IV

The fourth thing our frying-pan is saying to us is this. "What can't be cured must be endured." * What you cannot help, you have to take. What you cannot change, you have to stand. In other words, learn to make the best of all situations. Try to be happy where you *have to be*.

V

And the fifth and last thing the frying-pan is telling us runs like this. Joy and happiness are a state of mind. That is, real joy and real happiness are in your head; they are inside you; they come from within; they do not come from outside. *Do not depend on things.* Get joy from inside yourself. Do not look for it outside yourself. Don't depend on outside helps for happiness. Things outside you cannot make you happy if you are not going

* Francis Rabelais, 1495-1553: Works: Book v, Chap. xv. Also Robert Burton, 1576-1640: Anatomy of Melancholy: Part ii, Sect. 2, Memb. 3.

to be happy within. True and lasting happiness must come from inside. *FIND IT INSIDE YOURSELF.*

23

Keep It Sharp

❧

OBJECT: A razor blade.

❧

PERHAPS the boys and girls will recognize the object I hold in my hand this morning. How many of you do? Put up your hands! Yes, it is a razor blade. And I have brought it to church to show to you because I want to tell you a little story I once heard about a razor blade. A certain man was dressing one morning, getting ready for his breakfast and his day's work. He was shaving before the bathroom mirror and he seemed to be in some kind of trouble. He called to his wife and said:

" I cannot understand what is the matter with my razor this morning. It does not seem to work right at all. I thought my blade was sharp enough, but it seems as dull as dull can be. I don't understand it! " And to this his wife replied:

" It certainly ought to be sharp. It was sharp enough yesterday afternoon when I used it to cut the linoleum that I was fitting in the kitchen."

It was sharp enough the day before when his wife had used it to cut the linoleum. And she was wondering why it was not sharp enough the next day for shaving! You see, she had used the razor blade for a wrong purpose and in using it for a purpose for which it was never intended she had dulled the blade and spoiled it for shaving, for which purpose the blade had been made. She abused the blade and made it useless for its proper purpose. A razor blade must be kept sharp or it is of no use as a razor blade. Unless it is kept sharp it will not shave. It may cut linoleum but it will not do a good job on a man's face!

But a jack-knife blade must also be kept sharp if it is to do its job and do it properly. I once heard of a boy who had used the blade of his jack-knife as a can-opener. He was on a hike with some other boys. They wanted to open a can of baked beans. They had no can-opener. So the boy used his jack-knife blade and wondered ever afterward why it was so dull. I heard of another boy who was using his knife for a wrong purpose and broke one of the blades. He was throwing the knife, with open blade, toward a tree. The blade stuck in the tree. In getting it out, he broke it and left a large part of the blade forever stuck in the trunk of that tree. And ever afterward that blade was of no use to him. And I have even heard of a boy who had a knife with all the blades broken. That knife was not much good, was it?

So there are some things, like razor blades and knife blades, that we must keep sharp if we are going to use them and if they are going to do the things that we want them to do and the things that they are made to do. You cannot misuse a razor blade or a knife and expect to keep either one sharp and usable.

And just so it is with *conscience*. If your conscience is to be any good to you, you must keep it sharp. You know what your conscience is, don't you? It is that little voice inside of you that speaks to you when you start to do something wrong and tells you not to do it;

and that also speaks to you when you don't want to do something right and tells you that you must. Conscience is the voice of God inside our hearts. We know when conscience speaks to us. We all hear this voice of God. But the voice of conscience must be kept sharp or it will not do its proper work. It should be kept very sharp at all times, like a razor blade or a knife. If it gets dull we will not hear it so well, we will not pay so much attention to it, we will not profit by its speaking. For you must know that just as you can dull the sharpest razor blade or can spoil the sharpest knife, so you can dull conscience and spoil its little voice speaking to you at most important times, telling you not to do wrong and urging you to do right.

You can dull conscience by not listening to it. You can abuse conscience by not paying heed to it when it speaks. You can spoil conscience by not doing as it directs you to do. Don't dull your conscience. Don't abuse it. Keep it sharp!